Original title:
The Heart's Sweetest Rhythm

Copyright © 2025 Creative Arts Management OÜ
All rights reserved.

Author: Micah Sterling
ISBN HARDBACK: 978-3-69081-329-7
ISBN PAPERBACK: 978-3-69081-825-4

Dance of Devotion

Two left feet take the lead,
Wobbling like a clumsy steed,
Spinning wildly, laughter flies,
Chasing dreams beneath the skies.

Every shuffle brings a cheer,
Whirling friends both far and near,
In this dance, we find our bliss,
A joyful jig, we can't dismiss.

Tones of Togetherness

Banjos twang, a cat will sing,
While we all dance like puppets string,
With mismatched socks and silly hats,
We strut our stuff, like happy cats.

Each offbeat step a joyful tease,
Ticklish giggles float with ease,
In this melody we share the fun,
A bonding thread that can't be undone.

Rhapsody of Romance

With shoes too tight and shirts askew,
We fumble through sweet dances new,
A bump, a twist, a cheeky grin,
We trip and stumble, hearts to win.

Each clumsy turn, we laugh so loud,
Two oddball lovers, unswayed by crowd,
Under the stars, our quirks align,
In this goofy sway, your hand in mine.

Vibrations of Vitality

Jumpy beats make our knees quake,
With every laugh, the world will shake,
We jump so high, then fall so low,
Yet through it all, our spirits glow.

Like bouncing balls on trampoline,
Our joyful moves create a scene,
Laughter echoes, life's a song,
In this vibrant dance, we all belong.

Lifting Voices of Connection

In crowded rooms, we dance and sway,
With laughter loud and words at play.
A mishap here, a slip or two,
We'll never master this, it's true!

But every giggle breaks the ice,
We stumble forth, it feels so nice.
With every note, the mood aligns,
Creating bonds like silly vines.

The Language of Silent Yearning

A raised eyebrow, a wink or glance,
Turns awkward silence into dance.
We speak in smiles, a teasing game,
While two left feet refuse the blame.

With every blunder, a glance is shared,
Unspoken wishes, slightly unprepared.
A fumbled beat, but spirits soar,
In rhythm we'll be forever more!

Harmony Underneath the Veil

Beneath the cloak of laughter bright,
We find our groove, our sheer delight.
With silly jokes and random cheers,
We dance away our doubts and fears.

A wayward step, a twirl gone wrong,
Yet somehow still, we sing along.
The music plays, we act the fool,
In this grand dance, we make our rule!

A Cadence Woven in Dreams

In dreams, we leap like silly sprites,
With antics bold and grand delights.
Each twist and turn, a story spins,
In this odd waltz, we craft our wins.

A chaos here, a humorous fling,
We laugh so hard, our sides just sting.
In laughter's lift, we find our way,
As joy and whimsy lead the sway!

Love's Lyrical Whirlwind

In the dance of two, oh what a sight,
Spinning like tops, both day and night.
Your jokes are silly, your laughter's loud,
We trip through life, a bumbling crowd.

Our feet might falter, our steps askew,
But laughter finds us, and we giggle, too.
With every misstep, a memory made,
A love more vibrant, never to fade.

Notes of Joyful Reverie

Bouncing like beans, our spirits soar,
You snort when you laugh; oh, what a chore!
Your smile's a tune, all shiny and bright,
In this playful song, we take flight.

The coffee spills over—an artful spray,
Yet with the chaos, we dance, we play.
With each little blunder, we twirl and spin,
This goofy duet, where do we begin?

The Pulse of Togetherness

Two peas in a pod, we wobble and sway,
Catching our breath, and then we stray.
Your quirky charm makes the world seem right,
We laugh 'til we cry, into the night.

Your sock on my foot—how strange it feels,
Yet somehow, it's bliss, like unspoken deals.
Together we thrive in this wonderful mess,
A pulse that keeps beating, we surely confess.

Symphony of Heartfelt Moments

Our symphony starts with a hefty snore,
You wake with a jump, as I beg for more.
A fight for the blanket, a race for some toast,
In this sweet chaos, you are what I boast.

Each bite of our breakfast is accompanied by cheer,
As syrup spills over, we dodge it with glee.
The notes we compose are never quite right,
But that is our magic, our love's true delight.

Serenade of Tender Pulses

In the kitchen, pots go clank,
A dance-off starts, not a prank.
The cat joins in, with a flair,
Chasing shadows without a care.

We tap our feet, the rhythm's bright,
While socks slip here, oh what a sight!
Laughter echoes through the hall,
As we juggle love, not much at all.

Echoes of Affection's Song

Silly notes on napkins scrawled,
A serenade, yet we just bawled.
We each forgot the blender's hum,
Now smoothies look like sticky gum.

Under the stars, we skewer s'mores,
With laughter breaking down our doors.
The fire crackles, sparks take flight,
In this madness, everything feels right.

Secret Chords of Desire

Your weird dance moves, quite a show,
With twirls and dips, oh where'd you go?
A cake mix fight escalates fast,
Yet in this mess, we've found a blast.

With every sprinkles, giggles grow,
A secret code in frosting flow.
Our serenade's a sweet delight,
In silly chaos, we unite.

Pulse of Warm Embrace

The couch becomes our trampoline,
As laughter bursts like ice cream's sheen.
My jokes fly high, you roll your eyes,
Yet in your gaze, the fondness lies.

With playful nudges, we declare,
That silly moments fill the air.
A heartbeat shared in jestful tease,
In every giggle, love finds ease.

The Puzzle of Two Lives Entwined

In a café full of chatter, they clink their spoons,
Two tangled souls, dancing to cartoon tunes.
He spills his drink, she giggles with glee,
They play footsie beneath the old cherry tree.

His jokes are dad-like, her laughter a bell,
In a game of charades, he slips and he fell.
A spatula fly, with a wink and a cheer,
Together they tumble, love wrapped in a sneer.

They argue 'bout toppings on their pizza slice,
Is pineapple a fruit? Is it really so nice?
But she steals a bite, and they both start to grin,
In the kitchen of chaos, where the fun does begin.

With puzzles a-churning and laughter in tow,
Two lives intertwined, putting on their own show.
Through mishaps and hiccups, they find their own beat,
For the dance of their lives is oh-so-complete.

Rhapsody of Passionate Whispers

In the kitchen, love does gleam,
Burnt toast, yet we still beam.
Your dance moves, a comical sight,
Two left feet, yet you feel right.

With every laugh, our hearts collide,
In this chaos, we take pride.
You steal my fries, I steal your drink,
Together, we make hearts wink.

A serenade on the couch we share,
Buttons popping; do we care?
With snorts and giggles, we find our way,
In love's absurd, delightful play.

So here's to our silly sonnet's thread,
Where every mishap is joyously spread.
With playful jabs and goofy tunes,
We dance beneath the goofy moons.

Melodies of Soulful Connection

A serenade sung off-key,
Your shower voice is pure glee.
You hit the notes, your cat protests,
Paws over ears, it's quite the jest.

In this quirky little place,
We sing of love with no fine grace.
Your sock collection makes me laugh,
Odd patterns, it's a silly craft.

A pizza feast with toppings wild,
Tomato sauce goes flying, child!
With every bite, a little mess,
Our laughter rings—a sweet excess.

Hand in hand, we shimmy tight,
Spinning 'round till we lose sight.
Together in our funny dance,
No hearts can resist this chance.

Beating Beneath the Surface

Your snoring sounds like a bear's growl,
Yet near you, I can't help but howl.
Pajamas mismatched, oh what a sight,
Together we laugh, what pure delight.

Midnight snacks, a secret quest,
You steal the pie, I get the rest.
With crumbs all over, we start to grin,
This sweet mischief, let the games begin!

In this circus of quirks, we play,
Your silly puns brighten the day.
We build our dreams on a couch so wide,
With popcorn fights, we take our stride.

Through all the chaos, joy we find,
In laughter's rhythm, we unwind.
With playful moments lighting the way,
We dance through life, come what may.

A Song for Two Souls

In the park, we chase some geese,
Your dance moves invoke pure peace.
But when you trip, it's hard to breathe,
Laughter erupts, we can't deceive.

With ice cream cones that drip and slide,
We waddle like ducks, not a care inside.
Chocolate smudged on your cheek, it's true,
In our silly world, what's new?

We sing in the car like stars on stage,
Traffic lights stop, we're filled with rage.
Yet every honk brings out a smile,
It's a jolly ride in our funny style.

So let the music carry us far,
In this duet, you're my shining star.
With laughter, love, and silly dreams,
Together, we burst at the seams.

Symphony of Secrets

In the quiet of a bustling noon,
A cat plays piano, sings a tune.
The dogs are howling, joining in,
As squirrels dance with a cheeky grin.

A donut rolls down the slippery street,
Chased by a baker on tiny feet.
His frosting hat flies, a comic sight,
As laughter erupts in pure delight.

Whispers of cupcakes fill the air,
Each frosting swirl a secret to share.
The spoon sings tales of cookie dreams,
While chocolate rivers flow with beams.

In this cacophony of zany joy,
Even a broccoli finds a toy.
With a wink, the avocado jests,
As the beat of chaos never rests.

Poetics of Yearning

A pickle ponders its pickle jar,
Longing for freedom, to roam afar.
But every twist of the lid like fate,
Keeps it locked in a briny state.

A lonely sock wishes for its mate,
As it dances with an empty plate.
With a spin and a twirl, it dreams anew,
Of a laundry day with a vibrant crew.

The spaghetti sings to the meatball sphere,
"Join me in sauce, my dear, my dear!"
But the meatball rolls away in glee,
Chasing the garlic bread with glee.

Cookies and milk share heartfelt sighs,
As crumbs scatter under bright blue skies.
With a wink and a hug, they find their song,
In a pantry dance where all belong.

Notes of Nostalgia

In a world where socks have their say,
They reminisce about yesterday.
When the washing machine sang out loud,
And lint became a mischievous crowd.

A chair creaks tales of times gone by,
With cushions that giggle and sigh.
Remembering snacks that fell between,
As laughter echoed like a dream.

Bubblegum bubbles pop with cheer,
Sharing secrets only they can hear.
In the playground of yesterday's bliss,
They weave a tale with a fizzy kiss.

Old toys rally, dust them away,
For they still want to join the play.
With a rattle and a squeak, they find,
That joy's not lost, it's just rewind.

Flourish of Fervor

In the garden, the radish does a jig,
Next to a cabbage wearing a wig.
With colors that burst and bloom with flair,
They throw a party without a care.

The bees wear hats, all buzzing right,
Doing the cha-cha in joyous flight.
The flowers sway to the rhythm of bees,
As sunbeams dance through the leafy trees.

A tomato flirts with a green bean's twist,
While the lettuce winks, they can't resist.
Nature's concert, a flavorful jest,
With veggies laughing and feeling blessed.

In this garden, the fun won't cease,
As every sprout seeks a bit of peace.
Together they sway, a vibrant throng,
In a world where laughter sings along.

Swells of Affectionate Tide

When love's a wave, we ride so high,
A surfboard made of pumpkin pie.
With every splash, we laugh and cheer,
But watch out for that seagull near!

Our hearts do dance like jellyfish,
With twitchy moves that bring a wish.
Oh, how we twirl through salty air,
And share our snacks without a care!

In ocean depths, we lose our socks,
While building dreams with sandy blocks.
A tide of giggles pulls us close,
In this mad sea, we love the most!

As tide rolls back, we both take flight,
On boogie boards we share the night.
Splashing waves and silly grins,
This swells of joy, where laughter spins!

The Cadence of Endless Embrace

In a hug so wide, we both might freeze,
We cuddle close like two big cheese.
Our arms entwined, a pretzel twist,
We laugh so hard, we can't resist!

With every squeeze, a sound we make,
Like squeaky toys that giggle or shake.
A rhythm of joy, a jolly beat,
In this embrace, life's pretty sweet!

We dance around like clumsy fools,
Inventing new and funny rules.
Two bodies swaying, a wobbly sight,
Yet in this chaos, everything's right!

As daylight wanes, we plot and scheme,
To hug all night and build a dream.
With arms afire, and hearts so bold,
In our embrace, we never grow old!

Melodies of Light and Shadow

In shadows cast, we dance and prance,
With twinkling lights, it's quite a chance.
We sing off-key, yet loud and proud,
As echoes bounce, we draw a crowd!

Our laughter rings like silver bells,
In goofy tales, where magic dwells.
From silly socks to swaying hats,
Together we're the funniest spats!

With every note, a chuckle flows,
In rhythms strange, the friendship grows.
We skip through puddles, splash and shout,
A melody of giggles, there's no doubt!

Through ups and downs, we share our song,
In this duet, we can't go wrong.
With every beat, our spirits glow,
In light and shadow, love's the show!

The Tune of Everlasting Bonds

With every chord, we strike a laugh,
Like playful cats in a wooden staff.
Together we sing, with minor keys,
That echo through the swaying trees!

A harmony of funny faults,
In every note, a playful jolt.
We dance like ducks in silly shoes,
Creating chaos with funny moves!

In the background hums a friendly cheer,
As we croon songs only we can hear.
With every verse, our bond takes flight,
In this tune, we both feel right!

So grab your ukulele, let's unite,
In our joyful symphony tonight.
With laughter ringing, and hearts so fond,
We play this tune of endless bond!

The Soundtrack of Our Journey

We danced around the kitchen floor,
To the tunes of pots and pans galore.
A spatula mic in hand, oh what a show,
With every beat, our laughter did grow.

In the car, we sang off-key,
The GPS chimed in, "You missed the three!"
We turned it up, embraced the wrong,
Discovered harmony in our silly song.

The laundry basket, our stage divine,
As socks became stars, our clothes shined.
These quirky beats marked our days,
In giggles and mishaps, we found our ways.

From coffee spills to clumsy falls,
Life's remix played in crazy calls.
No orchestra needed, just you and me,
Creating a symphony of absurdity.

Enraptured by the Whispered Word

You told me secrets in a sly little way,
And I burst out laughing, "Is that here to stay?"
Each joke shared felt crucial and smart,
A witty whisper that tickled the heart.

With every sly grin and pun left to play,
We spun grand tales that would save the day.
From dragon snacks to pizza debates,
In this circus, we danced without traits.

For when you say, "I've had enough pie!"
I roll with laughter, give a cheeky sigh.
Words we uttered like wild little birds,
Each line was music without any chords.

Your laughter's a spell, I'm caught in your net,
In clever exchanges, we never forget.
So let's craft whispers, hilarious, free,
In this merry kingdom, just you and me.

Chasing Shadows of Euphoria

We raced through the night, adrenaline high,
With shadows as partners, we hugged the sky.
Chasing the laughter, slippery and bright,
Every small giggle felt just right.

With fireflies glowing, we misread the stars,
Thought we found treasure in candy bars.
A map made of crayon marked silly trails,
In our quest for joy, nothing else pales.

Yet somehow we tripped over a wild gopher,
Fell in the grass, then turned into loafers.
Our world was a playground of whimsical dreams,
Where laughter echoed in sunlit beams.

In every stumble, a tale to unfold,
Each moment rewoven, a comedy bold.
Caught in this chase, where shadows delight,
We'll wander forever, hearts taking flight.

Beats of Time in a Distant Night

Under moonlight, we pulled out the spoons,
Tap dancing softly with the stars and tunes.
A beat on the fridge, the clock counts our glee,
Each second a chorus, just you and me.

Laughter erupted at the faintest of sounds,
Every creak of the floorboard, wild joy abounds.
We wove tales of travel on a noodle-shaped track,
In our world of rhythm, there's no looking back.

The crickets joined in with their chirpy hums,
While we wrapped our heads in pretzel-like drums.
Silly rhythms escalated, it's a dance parade,
As life's sweet tempo got perfectly played.

In fleeting moments, we conquer the night,
Two playful hearts finding joy in the slight.
So let's drum our secrets, laughter so bright,
In this orchestra of chaos, we're twinkling light.

Euphony of Unbroken Silence

In quiet rooms where whispers dance,
A sneeze erupts, breaks perfect chance.
The silence shatters, laughter flows,
As dust bunnies join in, who knows?

A cat leaps up with regal grace,
And knocks down books, a grand disgrace.
The rhythm's off, yet none complain,
For chaos sings a sweet refrain.

We hum a tune of muted glee,
As spoons play jazz in harmony.
The clock ticks loud, a mismatched beat,
Yet here we find our joyful seat.

With every quirk the night unfolds,
A symphony of laughter molds.
In moments strange, we find our song,
In wiggles, giggles, where we belong.

Harmonizing Souls

Two quirky friends, a cheeky duo,
With songs of socks and dancing shoos.
They strum the air like silly fools,
And dream of breaking all the rules.

A pie flies past, a whipped cream dream,
They laugh so hard, they cannot scream.
Their voices blend, like cats that croon,
A melody beneath the moon.

With mismatched tunes and offbeat sways,
They find their joy in silly ways.
A chorus of zest, a playful cheer,
Together they hold fun so dear.

In every jest, a secret note,
A playful jab, a friendly quote.
Their harmony is never planned,
A wild concert, hand in hand.

The Maelstrom of Passion's Touch

In tangled sheets a brawl begins,
With pillow fights and tickling spins.
Two lovers clash with garden gnomes,
Inventing songs of travel homes.

A spat turns into playful wit,
As one retreats and then they flit.
They dance around with laughter true,
In this whirlwind of silly view.

The kitchen's splattered, oh my dear!
A cereal shower, isn't it clear?
With every splash, a giggle grows,
In this wild storm, pure love glows.

They sing of quirks and stolen fries,
With every note a sweet surprise.
Their hearts collide a joyous crash,
In a maelstrom of love's wild splash.

Merging Melodies at Sunset

As day turns gold, a tune unwinds,
With silly songs and jumbled lines.
At sunset's grace, the world does sway,
In harmony of childlike play.

A dog trots by with wiggly flair,
While squirrels join in, without a care.
The breezes hum, a soft refrain,
As laughter echoes, like a train.

Two hearts collide, each pun a treasure,
In mismatched steps, they find their pleasure.
A twirl, a giggle, a playful chase,
In every moment, they find their space.

With every note that swirls and dips,
They seal their fate with silly quips.
The sun dips low, the music spins,
In merging tunes, the magic begins.

Rhythms of Resilience

Life's a dance, we stumble and sway,
Knees are sore, but we laugh anyway.
With every misstep, we twirl and we spin,
In this wacky waltz, joy's always a win.

Pizza toppings tossed like confetti on air,
We groove in the kitchen, no rhythm, just flair.
Juggling our troubles, we trip, we might fall,
But laughter echoes; it's the best beat of all.

Crescendo of Comradeship

Friends gather 'round, like notes in a chord,
Strumming life's strings, with a loud, raucous roar.
A harmony built on inside jokes and glee,
With each silly blunder, we sing loud and free.

Swinging our arms, as if we could fly,
We dance on the table, oh my, oh my!
In the chaos of joy, we find our refrain,
Making memories sweet, like a sugarcane.

Aria of Affectionate Souls

Two quirky hearts, with a beat all their own,
Dancing through days, in a rhythm well-known.
With every high note, and low plunk they sing,
A duet of laughter, like spring's playful fling.

Sharing secrets, like a melody's tease,
Tickling each other, always aiming to please.
When life hits a sour note—just chuckle and sway,
Together, we twirl through the wildest ballet.

Ballad of Unspoken Bonds

A glance, a nudge, the humor's implied,
In silence we share, like a rollercoaster ride.
No need for grand speeches or words of the wise,
Our friendship's a tune that always complies.

Like socks with holes, we embrace the odd sights,
Living our lives in mismatched delights.
With every shared giggle, our spirits take flight,
In the song of the silly, we find pure delight.

Soundtrack of Sentiments

When love's a song, we sing it loud,
With goofy notes to make us proud.
A melody of clumsy grace,
In every laugh, we find our place.

The saxophone's a wiggly beast,
It plays our hearts in a wild feast.
While ukuleles strum our dreams,
And bubblegum pops with silly beams.

Our love's a tune, both bright and strange,
Like dancing squirrels, the rhythms change.
A jingle here, a funky twist,
In every beat, we can't resist.

So let's duet in silly glee,
With catchy hooks for you and me.
In every chord, a joke we share,
With laughter echoing everywhere.

Mirth in Minor Keys

In minor keys, we trip and fall,
Our laughter bounces off the wall.
With every fumble, joy ignites,
We spin in circles, in fits and flights.

A tuba toots a comical tune,
As dancing penguins join our swoon.
With each offbeat, we trip and glide,
In humor's lap, we take our ride.

A song of giggles, off and on,
Like magic carpets, here and gone.
In awkward rhymes, we find our way,
As silly thoughts come out to play.

So let the music flow and sway,
As we get lost in our ballet.
For in these laughs, we'll find the clue,
To love's own dance, both bright and new.

Interlude of Intimacy

In moments shared, we whisper soft,
Like kittens playing, we drift aloft.
Our secrets hum in playful tones,
With giggles mixing, heartbeats moans.

A serenade of silly fears,
Our banter trickles like fine beers.
In cozy corners, we exchange
The quirks and quips that feel so strange.

With crumpled notes and doodled lines,
We chart our dreams with laugh-filled signs.
Each awkward pause, a canvas bright,
Painting our joys in soft moonlight.

So let the world outside take flight,
We'll dance together, hearts delight.
For in this space, with jest and glee,
We find the sweetest intimacy.

Pulse of Possibilities

Tick-tock goes the clock of fate,
A rhythm strange, we celebrate.
With silly steps and offbeat grins,
We dive right in, where laughing begins.

Each pulse a chance to take the lead,
To jump and twirl, to plant a seed.
In every misstep, joy's parade,
With pratfalls and trips, our plans are made.

A symphony of whims and dreams,
Improbable schemes bursting at the seams.
With silly hats and worn-out shoes,
We sketch our futures, laugh, and choose.

So let's embrace this rhythmic game,
With crazy beats, we fan the flame.
For in this dance of pure delight,
Our hearts beat loud, both day and night.

Dances in the Soft Dawn Light

In the morning, I twirl so bright,
Birds join in, what a silly sight!
My pajamas flapping like wings,
Who knew sunrise had such things?

Coffee's brewing, a dance-off spree,
Spilling some grounds, oh woe is me!
Every sip comes with a jig,
I feel like a big dancing pig!

Cats join in with a graceful pounce,
To the couch, they bounce and bounce!
Together we prance, all in mirth,
Celebrating the joy of this earth!

Sunlight streaming through the trees,
I sway in breeze with giggles and wheezes!
Morning mayhem, a funny sight,
Dancing boisterously till it's night!

A Song Painted in Colors of Love

With a palette bright, I start to sing,
Splatters of paint, oh, what a fling!
Colors collide, a wonderful mess,
Who knew love could cause such distress?

Canvases fly, and brushes do too,
As my cat rolls in the vibrant hue!
With laughter that echoes through the air,
Creating a masterpiece beyond compare!

Smudged faces from paint in the fray,
We giggle and laugh, oh what a display!
Each stroke tells a tale, each shade a tease,
In the rhythm of joy, hearts learn to please!

The sun dips low, colors fade away,
Yet the laughter lingers, come what may!
In this symphony of colorful glee,
Love's funny dance is the masterpiece spree!

Beacons of Eternal Connection

Two socks in a drawer, what a pair,
One's always missing, can you declare?
They giggle in silence, a cozy embrace,
Dancing together in their little space!

When the doorbell rings, they know it's time,
For a sock hop, oh so sublime!
With feet tapping, they jump out with flair,
Annoying my neighbors; they just don't care!

In mismatched styles, they find their groove,
Slipping and sliding, making us move!
A beacon of joy in the laundry heap,
Creating connections that make us leap!

So here's to the socks, bright and free,
Who dance on our floors, what a sight to see!
In this funny rhythm, our hearts connect,
With every step, we can self-reflect!

Tapestry of Heartfelt Verses

We weave our tales with silly threads,
Stitching together laughter that spreads!
Patchwork of moments, bright and bizarre,
Every knot tied with a giggly spark!

From the tales of mishaps at every turn,
To the funny things that we all learn!
Each verse a reflection of moments shared,
In the fabric of life, our spirits flared!

My dog steals my socks, leaves me in plight,
Yet, we both cackle with pure delight!
Every thread of laughter holds us tight,
In this tapestry, the world's so bright!

So let's gather our yarns, let humor reign,
In this quilt of memories, joy will remain!
With verses stitched in the softest hues,
We dance through life with love and a muse!

Notes from the Chamber of Love

In the room where giggles bloom,
A sock puppet steals the show,
With silly jokes and a happy boom,
It dances like a clown in tow.

Love's a game of charades played,
With faux pas and laughs galore,
Each blunder comes with a serenade,
And every stumble, we adore.

Candy hearts on a windy day,
Tangled in fun, we twirl and spin,
Like silly kids at a bright ballet,
Where laughter is the prize to win.

Together we make a wacky team,
Juggling joy like a circus show,
In the land where absurdity beams,
Our sweetest notes begin to flow.

Rhythm of Night's Caress

In the moonlight, shadows dance,
As crickets play with glee,
A raccoon steals a fateful glance,
As if it knows love's spree.

Stars twinkle, bringing a laugh,
While owls hoot a surprise,
A firefly does a sultry half,
It glows with sparkly eyes.

We sway to the rhythm of night,
With goofy moves and silly grins,
Underneath the soft starlight,
Where all best fun begins.

A serenade from frogs nearby,
Their croaks, a playful song,
As we share stories, oh so spry,
In this night where we belong.

Echoes in the Stillness

Echoes bounce off walls so bright,
As we chuckle and relate,
A whisper turns into delight,
Our laughter, it resonates.

In the stillness, shadows play,
With tickles and friendly jests,
Silly secrets lead the way,
Each giggle, a winning quest.

Laughter weaves a magic thread,
Spinning tales that make us roar,
As we recall the things we said,
In this game we both adore.

From echoes rise our silly dreams,
In the quiet moments of bliss,
With heartbeats joined in laughter's beams,
Each whisper, a playful kiss.

Chimes of Enchanted Affection

When chimes ring out with glee,
Silly tunes fill the air,
We dance like leaves from a tree,
Creating fun everywhere.

Each jingle brings a giggle spree,
Marshmallow clouds pass over head,
As we jump like bumblebees,
With no worries, no dread.

From rooftops, laughter spills,
Like confetti in the breeze,
With every note, pure joy fulfills,
In a rhythm that never flees.

Together we strum our hearts' strings,
In this festival of light,
As just being us sings,
The chimes of love ignite.

Lyric of Life's Embrace

Life's a tune, so fun and bright,
Dancing under the disco light.
With every giggle, a step we take,
Bumping our heads, oh what a mistake!

In the kitchen, spoons start to clang,
As we cook, the cat does hang.
Adding spices, a pinch of cheer,
While my partner hums, 'Oh dear, oh dear!'

Grocery carts race down the aisle,
With every turn, we meet a smile.
The checkout line becomes our stage,
As we perform, releasing our rage!

So here's to laughter, the best of tunes,
In the chaos, dance with the loons.
Life's a song, let's sing it loud,
With quirky steps and laughter, we're proud!

Essence in Every Beat

Pulsing rhythms in morning's light,
Coffee brews, a joyful sight.
My socks do vanish into thin air,
Even they can't handle this flair!

Stumbling out in mismatched pairs,
People chuckle, their pointing glares.
Yet I spin with a grin so wide,
Who's got time for silly pride?

Picnic days with ants on parade,
As we feast on crumbs I made.
Laughter echoes, food takes flight,
Our playful banter brings pure delight!

So dance through life's whimsical beat,
Embrace the rhythm, stick with the beat.
With every trip and playful fall,
We weave a song that enchants us all!

Whispers of Love's Melody

Two hearts twirl like partners divine,
As I slip on pie-soaked spine.
A serenade where humor reigns,
To twinkle toes and silly gains.

Your laughter's the music I crave,
Though you steal the covers, not so brave.
With pillows tossed and blankets tight,
A nightly ruckus, what a sight!

Whispers soft, the clock ticks slow,
In our dance, we steal the show.
Even the cat joins our spree,
As we tango, quite clumsily!

So sway with me through life so grand,
With quirky moves and laughter planned.
Together we hum, a tune so sweet,
In the chaos, our love's upbeat!

Dance of the Silent Beat

In the quiet, we weave our song,
With silent laughs, righting the wrong.
Footsteps shuffle in comic style,
An unspoken dance that makes us smile!

A wink from you, a playful glance,
Inviting me to share this dance.
Though our rhythm may seem askew,
Who can resist this waltz with you?

Even the fridge joins in the beat,
As we sway around, oh what a feat!
The dog barks on cue for flair,
While we spin like we just don't care!

So let's trip and tumble through the day,
With every misstep, come what may.
In our quirky steps, let's find our talk,
In the dance of life, let's boldly walk!

Symphony of Fleeting Moments

In a dance of tripping feet,
We stumble over love so sweet.
A slip, a fall, a burst of cheer,
Who knew romance had such a rear?

With giggles shared at awkward stares,
We compose tunes, forget our cares.
A serenade of silly notes,
As laughter ties our love with ropes.

We joke about the odds we take,
On sunny days, or when it's fake.
For every pratfall, joy will sway,
The sweetest tune, in silly play.

So here's to chaos, fun, and glee,
A symphony of you and me.
We'll waltz through life, be it a dance,
And laugh aloud at each mischance.

Echoing in the Void

In empty rooms, our voices sing,
We echo back what chaos brings.
A yelp, a sneeze, a rolling laugh,
In silent halls, we're quite the staff.

Every joke that slips our lips,
Like playful ducks on funny trips.
In quiet nights, we stir the air,
With echoes loud, we're quite the pair.

The stillness breaks with quips and jives,
We fill the void, oh how it thrives!
With playful nudges, rollicking cheer,
Our symphony is loud and clear.

We share the sounds that hug the walls,
The way we laugh when duty calls.
In empty spaces, our joy's deployed,
Together still, in void, enjoyed.

The Resonance of Gentle Touch

A poke, a nudge, a playful hit,
Our fingers dance, they never quit.
With silly taps, we tease and play,
A gentle touch, our own ballet.

In moments brief, our laughter swells,
It bounces off the walls like bells.
With winks and nods, we start a duel,
In tender games, we're just plain fools.

The way you tickle, I howl with glee,
In this soft battle, you're tough on me.
Each poke is sweet, each pinch a song,
Oh how this harmony feels so wrong!

Yet in these jests, we softly weave,
A warm embrace, you best believe.
With silly touches, life's a rush,
In playful moments, there's no hush.

An Ode to Timeless Affection

An ancient love, yet oh so new,
We prance around, just me and you.
With clumsy moves, we slip and slide,
Yet hand in hand, we'll always glide.

Through tangled sheets and messy hair,
We laugh aloud, without a care.
An ode to us, a merry song,
Where goofy moments just belong.

While candles melt, we dance in light,
Our shadows play, a comical sight.
With every chuckle, love's on display,
In endless jest, we're here to stay.

So raise a glass, let's toast this cheer,
For in this laughter, you are dear.
With joyful jabs, we hum along,
An endless tune that feels like strong.

Timeless Dance of Beating Hearts

In a waltz of socks and shoes,
We twirl and spin, dodging blues.
With each step, a giggle sneaks,
As we embrace our rhythm's peaks.

Chocolate stains upon the floor,
Dance partners shout, 'One more encore!'
We leap and glide, flamboyant crew,
In this ruckus, love feels brand new.

A tuba honks our silly tune,
As owls outside hoot at the moon.
With every beat our laughter swells,
Our dance a story that joy tells.

So here we go, the night is bright,
With twinkling lights, our pure delight.
An endless jig, we'll never part,
In this ballet of the living heart.

The Melody of Shared Secrets

Whispers travel like the breeze,
Over cupcakes, under trees.
Giggling softly, hearts collide,
In each secret, we confide.

The memes we share, a silly bunch,
Make even broccoli taste like lunch.
With every laugh, a tale unfolds,
An orchestra of joy retold.

Underneath the starlit skies,
We craft our jokes, the greatest prize.
With every chuckle, bonds constrict,
A melody that we depict.

Our symphony, a playful flight,
Echoes softly into the night.
With a wink, our secrets spread,
Life's a tune we've always led.

Lullabies of Intimate Communion

In kitchens swirling with delight,
We clap our hands and dance at night.
Cookies crumbling, giggles soar,
As we hum just a little more.

Two left feet when we attempt,
To make a spell that time exempt.
Plates are flying through the air,
Yet laughter heals our little scare.

Tickle fights and silly dreams,
We sing our hopes in strange regimes.
The chaos holds a sweet embrace,
In every mishap, find our place.

When light fades and stars align,
We whisper jokes; they age like wine.
In our rhythm, life's serenade,
The lullabies of fun are made.

Rhythms of Forgotten Dreams

Naps are sneaky, dreams are wild,
In toddler beds, I'm still a child.
With every snore, the dog joins in,
A harmony where giggles begin.

Chasing shadows that click and clap,
In this circus, we find a map.
With every stumble, we break the mold,
In ancient rhythms that we're bold.

Banana peels and silly hats,
We leap and sing with all the cats.
Each mishap leads to jolly cheer,
In forgotten tunes, we dance near.

As the sun sets, laughter blooms,
In this dance of joy, forget the glooms.
For every heartbeat brings a dream,
In rhythm, we find our silly theme.

Cadence of Intimate Dreams

In the dance of silly thoughts,
My socks don't match, oh, what a plot!
Stumbling over dreams we weave,
Laughs shared in a world we leave.

Tickling fancies float like clouds,
Whispered giggles in crowded crowds.
Balloons we chase, they slip and fly,
Hopes bounce high, like popcorn in the sky.

Waltzing through our clumsy fears,
Embracing joy with silly cheers.
Underneath the moon's bright glow,
Twinkle toes in a feathery show.

In a realm of playful bliss,
A squirrel's dance we can't dismiss.
With quirks that make our spirits swell,
In laughter's arms, we cast our spell.

Vibrations in the Twilight

As evening paints the sky with hue,
A cat sneezes—bless you, too!
Sidewalks hum a funny tune,
While fireflies jiggle 'neath the moon.

Mismatched slippers chase a beat,
Rabbits hop and skip on street.
The trees sway with a giggling breeze,
Swapping secrets with buzzing bees.

A dance-off with a wayward crow,
He thinks he's smooth, but oh, the show!
In twilight's laughter, dreams take flight,
Echoes of joy linger through the night.

Each chuckle weaves a tale of glee,
As shadows twirl with chivalry.
Under stars that laugh and wink,
We find rhythm in a playful blink.

Harmonies of Unspoken Longing

With whispers of wishes tucked away,
Clumsy strides in an awkward ballet.
A toad croaks bold romance at dark,
While a tree branch steals the spotlight's spark.

Twinkling eyes and silly grins,
Frogs in tuxedos and spinning sins.
Seagulls squawk with secret dreams,
As laughter bursts in vibrant streams.

The sun sets low on spaghetti nights,
Pasta dances in clumsy bites.
In the muddle of unplanned fate,
A rhyming heart knows how to wait.

With each chuckle, longing plays,
A serenade of goofy ways.
And in the mix of dreams that twine,
The melody is sweet, and so divine.

Gentle Beats Beneath the Stars

Under starlit skies, we sway,
Tickling wishes, come what may!
A playful breeze, a buzz of fun,
And unexpected splashes from a run.

Pigeons strut with swaggered flair,
Wobbling joy in the evening air.
As laughter echoes, shadows blend,
Dancing steps that never end.

Whimsical dreams twirl overhead,
Chasing giggles, we are led.
With moonlit glances, smiles retire,
Each heartbeat sparks our silly fire.

In every flutter, each playful glance,
Life's too short not to dance!
So let's celebrate these quirky art,
And find the beat that steals the heart.

Touch of Reverberating Love

In a land of socks and shoes,
We dance like we've got nothing to lose.
With each silly twirl, we bump and collide,
But laughing together, we set our pride.

A spoon in my coffee, your spoon in mine,
Stirring up trouble, tasting divine.
We giggle and snort, in a whirlwind we spin,
Love's likelier source? The chocolate within.

Like ants on a march, we march in a line,
You step on my toe, I say, 'Is that fine?'
With our noses in books, sometimes making a mess,
We've made reading a sport—don't put it to test!

So let the clumsy rhythms hit the floor,
As we dance with our mishaps, always wanting more.
With laughter like thunder, bent over we're bent,
In this mad little jig, our love is content.

The Sound of Heartstrings in Harmony

Your snore is a tune, my morning alarm,
With a chorus of hiccups, there's never a harm.
We harmonize well, though the notes go awry,
Like cats with a piano—oh my, oh my!

I trip on your slippers, you steal all my fries,
Yet together we laugh at our own silly cries.
We dance to the symphony of the mundane,
Every spilled drink is our own little gain.

The washing machine sings as it spins all our clothes,
Together we giggle at the laundry that grows.
Music in loud silence, no rhythm you see,
In this cacophony, there's only you and me.

So here's to our laughter, our off-beat parade,
In the mess of it all, our tune never fades.
With a wink and a smile, our melody's grand,
A playful serenade, always hand in hand.

Rhythmic Echoes of Togetherness

In the kitchen, you dance and I chop,
You step on the cat, he gives a loud yelp.
Mixing ingredients, a sprinkle of fun,
Our culinary concert has just begun.

We pick up the beat with a tap and a slide,
Your flour explosion takes me for a ride.
The cookies won't bake, but our hearts surely do,
With each laugh we share, I just can't be blue.

Coffee spills over; it splatters the wall,
Who knew our mornings could glitter and fall?
We dance through the chaos, oh what a wild show,
In the sweetest calamity, our true feelings grow.

So here's to the rhythm of life and of pie,
With a spoon as a baton, we reach for the sky.
Each echo of laughter a note in our song,
Together, dear love, where we both belong.

A Duet of Delighted Souls

Your socks are mismatched, mine are in flair,
We strut like peacocks without any care.
The world's our stage; our audience? None,
With a quirk in our hearts, we dance just for fun.

When we share our snacks, what a joyous plight,
You hide the good ones like they're a great sight.
With a wink and a grin, the crumbs fly around,
Together we soar, on this sweet merry ground.

In the chaos of life, we find a suave groove,
With a twist and a shout, oh how we move!
Every day is a jest, wrapped in our spree,
In this duet of love, we're utterly free.

So keep up your antics, I'll add my delight,
We'll laugh through the stumbles, creating new heights.
With a jive in the air and a spark in our souls,
In this tune of togetherness, our laughter rolls.

Flows of Affectionate Light

In the morning sun we dance,
Chasing shadows, what a chance!
With giggles bright and silly ways,
We juggle love like sunny rays.

Butterflies join in our cheer,
Spreading laughter far and near.
We twirl like leaves caught in a breeze,
In this joy, we're sure to please.

A tickle fight beneath the trees,
You make me laugh, oh, yes, you tease!
Like ice cream drips on a warm day,
Sweet moments melt, come what may.

When stars appear, we steal the show,
With goofy smiles, our faces glow.
Affection flows like soda pop,
In our world, we'll never stop!

Resonating Souls in Dusk

Underneath an orange sky,
We burst out laughing, oh my, oh my!
A dance-off with a lamp post tall,
You groan but love my silly call.

Cactus friends in a wild spree,
Join our party, can't you see?
We share mischief with the stars,
And dance like we've won fancy cars.

With fireflies glowing, we conspire,
To make a joy-buzz, never tire.
A cookie jar, our secret stash,
Let's scoff them down, oh what a bash!

As night descends, our laughter gleams,
Dancing souls in offbeat dreams.
In this moment, life is sweet,
With you, my friend, I'm complete!

The Melody in Each Breath

Sipping tea and watching cats,
Who think they're great acrobats.
With every sip, we trade a smile,
We're clocking fun, it's worth the while.

Eating cake in silly hats,
You tease, I giggle – how 'bout that?
Our breaths sync like a funny song,
Perfectly offbeat, where we belong.

From every corner, laughter rolls,
Like marching bands with rubber soles.
Our thoughts collide like playful flies,
Creating joy that never dies.

In the quiet, whispers play,
Every moment, a new ballet.
Together, we breathe a lighter tune,
Underneath the laughing moon!

Chords of Unending Devotion

With rubber ducks, we start the show,
In our bathtub where giggles flow.
Each splash a note, a silly cheer,
Together we conquer laughter's sphere.

Playing cards, you steal my ace,
With funny faces, we embrace space.
In every jest, our spirits sing,
Inside this joy, we reign as kings.

From pancake flipping to crazy socks,
We craft our jokes like building blocks.
In this orchestra of delight,
Love's melodies shine in the night.

Forever bound in playful schemes,
You're my favorite in all my dreams.
With humor's spark, our hearts take flight,
In this laughter, everything feels right!

Pulses of Passion

In a dance where socks don't match,
Two left feet with quite a catch.
We trip and laugh, it's all a game,
An awkward jig, but who's to blame?

With pizza crumbs upon our shirts,
We tango, twirl, and jump in spurts.
Each giggle adds a beat that's bold,
A rhythm forged in tales retold.

As hearts collide at awkward bends,
We might not win, but we have friends.
In laughter's echo, sweet as pie,
Our feet may falter, but spirits fly.

So here we sway in laughter's light,
With silly moves that feel just right.
Our friends may laugh, but that's okay,
We dance our way through every day.

Whispers of Love

I whisper sweet nothings each night,
While you snore loud, what a delight!
Your dreams of cheese, oh, how they sing,
In a world where mice wear crowns, they fling!

A love note slipped under your plate,
Scribbled on napkins, it's quite the fate.
You find it while munching on fries,
With ketchup stains like sweet surprise.

In this circus of quirks and grins,
Love's comedy glory always wins.
With tickles and pranks, we stitch our fate,
The show must go on, can't miss a date!

So here's to whispers and silly days,
In our joyful, peculiar ways.
With laughter like balloons in the sky,
Our love's a jest that will never die.

Cadence of Connection

We drop the beat with clumsy hands,
A symphony of misfit bands.
With spoons as drums, we make a sound,
As laughter bounces all around.

Your jokes hit notes that go amiss,
But somehow still, we find our bliss.
We ride the rhythm of our dreams,
Like wobbly bikes on silly beams.

In the dance of meals we share,
Spaghetti flung through the air,
Our sauce-stained shirts tell tales so bright,
Of all the ways we find delight.

So here's to the moments that make us laugh,
In our goofy, giddy parade we quaff.
With each clumsy step, we'll strut and play,
In this wild groove, we'll find our way.

Serenade of Solitude

In solitude, I wear a crown,
A solo act, I won't back down.
My pet goldfish judges my moves,
He giggles with bubbles, approving grooves.

With satirical songs, I serenade,
The cat rolls her eyes, in the shade.
My dance floor's a kitchen rug,
Where I spin alone in my coffee mug.

The fridge hums back with a steady beat,
As I warble tunes with my own two feet.
Who needs a partner? I'm quite the star,
In this solo show, I raise the bar!

So lift your glass to the quirky calm,
Where solitude drips like a sweet balm.
I may dance alone, but it's always fun,
In this serenade, I've already won!

Beats of Belonging

In a crowded room, I sway,
Tapping toes, a dance ballet.
Friends, they giggle, steal the show,
Two left feet, but here we go!

Laughter rings with every beat,
A rhythm that's both light and sweet.
We spin around, just lost in time,
Who knew that clumsiness could rhyme?

With silly hats and quirky moves,
No judge in sight, just silly grooves.
Each shared glance, our joy ignites,
As laughter echoes through the nights.

So dance with me, your heart's a drum,
Let's shake the floor till morning comes.
In every stumble, every cheer,
We find our home, we're glad to be here!

Songs of Surrender

With a sigh, I drop my guard,
In the kitchen, here's my bard.
Singing off-key with all my might,
Pasta boiling, what a sight!

Neighbors laugh at my crooning tune,
While the cat howls like a loon.
With every note, I spill the sauce,
A chef's delight—oh, what a loss!

Dancing round with spoons in hand,
Making music—quite unplanned.
Each blunder builds a laughter chord,
In my kitchen, fun's restored.

So let me sway and hum along,
In this chaos, I belong.
With every dish, a memory spun,
In my kitchen, surrender's fun!

Chords of Contentment

A lazy day, the sun's so bright,
In fuzzy socks, it feels just right.
Couch-potato mode is on,
As snacks and smiles tip the dawn.

Remote control, a battle to claim,
With rivals here, it's all a game.
Flip through channels, what a mess,
In our chaos, we find success.

Each joke we share, a gentle tear,
Who knew boredom could bring cheer?
So here's to naps and silly memes,
Our cozy world's the stuff of dreams.

In this melody of lazy fun,
We're content, we've just begun.
With every chuckle, life feels grand,
In these chords, together we stand!

Resonance of Desire

With pizza in hand and a grin so wide,
We share our dreams, no need to hide.
Whispers float, like cheesy strings,
In this laughter, my heart sings.

We plot and scheme for future days,
In our fantasies, a quirky maze.
Each silly wish, a giggle shared,
In our banter, we've both dared.

Late night talks with dreams so grand,
In this chaos, we take a stand.
Every joke, a spark we share,
With every chuckle, we're almost there.

So let's embrace this silly dance,
In goofy chats, we'll take a chance.
Each moment shared, a spark of fire,
In our laughter lies desire.

A Ballad Written in the Stars

In the sky, I spotted a cow,
Dancing up there, what a wow!
It twirled with grace, such a scene,
Mooing to the stars, like a queen.

The sheep joined in with a jig,
Looking so cute, yet quite big.
Around they spun, in the night,
Filling the sky with pure delight.

A cat in a hat sang a tune,
To the light of the silvery moon.
With all this chaos, who would guess,
That love could thrive in such a mess?

So take a chance, grab a snack,
Join the dance, don't hold back.
For when the stars begin to play,
A love ballad warms the day.

Whirls of Sweet Surrender

A duck in boots went for a glide,
With every waddle, joy supplied.
It spun around with silly flair,
Quacking loudly without a care.

The breeze then joined for a laugh,
Tickling tails with its gentle staff.
They whirled together, made quite a pair,
With laughter ringing through the air.

A turtle tried to join the game,
But moved so slow, it felt like shame.
Yet every twirl, he watched with glee,
Thinking, "One day, that'll be me!"

So let's all whirl, with grace and zest,
In the rhythm of fun, we're all blessed.
Surrender to silly, let it shine,
In the world of laughter, your heart's divine.

Serene Beats of Moonlit Echoes

A hedgehog danced in moonlit glow,
Spinning round and round, oh so slow.
He pricked the ground with tiny feet,
In a rhythm that was quite a treat.

The frogs croaked out a lively beat,
As crickets tapped their little feet.
Together they sang a funny song,
Echoing dreams where all belong.

A firefly flashed, dancing near,
Winking to the moon, never fear.
With every flicker, the night would shine,
In this playful realm, love intertwines.

So hold on tight, don't let it slip,
Join the dance, give joy a trip.
For in the echoes, where laughter flows,
Magic awaits, and love surely grows.

A Love Song Carried by the Breeze

A squirrel sat high in a tree,
Playing a tune so wild and free.
With acorns swaying, a sweet refrain,
He sang of love in the soft rain.

The wind took hold of his sweet verse,
Whispering notes, like a playful curse.
It tickled flowers, made them sway,
Turning each moment into play.

A parrot joined with laughter bright,
Repeating lines through the starry night.
With every squawk, a wink was thrown,
As love danced on in tones well-known.

So let the breeze steal your cares,
And weave a song that serenely flairs.
For in each giggle, in every tease,
Love finds a way, like a playful breeze.

Melodies of Affection

I took a step, you took a dance,
Your left foot tripped, I missed my chance.
We twirled and whirled through the café's flare,
Coffee spilled down, splashed everywhere!

A serenade by a cat named Lou,
He purred, and we laughed like a silly crew.
With rhythm so weird, yet hearts still light,
We danced like fools into the night.

You hummed a tune, a curious sound,
A parrot cawed back from the ground.
With feathers and laughter, we made quite the scene,
In this funny rhythm, we felt so keen.

So here's to the jests and the giggles we share,
Life's silly dance will always be fair.
With each little step, we craft our own song,
In the quirkiest way, where we both belong.

Echoes of Embrace

Your hug's a storm in a teacup small,
Squeezing me tight, do I hear a call?
Like a duck in a bowtie, I quack in surprise,
These silly embraces bring tears to my eyes.

We danced round the room with mismatched socks,
This twirly whirl with a few wedged rocks.
You spun me around till I tumbled down,
Of course, a raucous laugh was the only sound.

With a wink and a grin, my foot slipped away,
You chuckled and said, "That's how we play!"
Echoes of laughter fill up the space,
In this bond we share, there's no slower pace.

So let's sway to this rhythm, so odd and bright,
Two quirky hearts dancing through the night.
With a bit of chaos, we find our embrace,
Creating sweet echoes of love's funny trace.

Harmonies of Tenderness

In a world that's a merry-go-round of fun,
Our quirks play together like laughter begun.
You step on my toes, I elbow you back,
This melody's funny, there's no need to pack.

Like a blender mishap, we whirl and we shake,
Every goofy twist is a joyful mistake.
Our harmony's made from the quirkiest bits,
With laughter that bubbles and never quite quits.

You sing out of key, oh, what a delight!
Yet here we are jiving, our spirits take flight.
The laughter, it dances on every wrong note,
We sail through this symphony, keep it afloat.

So let together make a ruckus today,
With silly eyed winks and our own ballet.
In the sweetest of rhythms, we'll cling and we'll sway,
Two hearts in the chorus, come what may.

Lullabies of Longing

Under the stars, we're chasing a dream,
With stargaze battles and wild ice cream.
You tug at my sleeve in a curious mood,
Whispers of wishes, oh, this is good!

As we frolic around like balloons in the park,
Each laugh and each smile ignites a spark.
On swings that seem higher than mountains we climb,
In our childlike heartbeats, there's rhythm and rhyme.

Like a cat on a fence with a curious stare,
I ponder and wander, wonder what's fair.
Shall we leap into laughter or sail on a whim?
In lullabies soft, let's dance on the rim.

So here's for the giggles, for all that we share,
In the sweetest embrace of a funny affair.
With rhythms of longing wrapped up in delight,
We'll dance through the echoes, hearts full and bright.